WIND ON THE HEATH

WIND ON THE HEATH

new and selected poems by
NAOMI BETH WAKAN

Shanti Arts Publishing
Brunswick, Maine

WIND ON THE HEATH
New and Selected Poems

Published by Shanti Arts Publishing
Interior and cover design by Shanti Arts Designs

Shanti Arts LLC
193 Hillside Road
Brunswick, Maine 04011
shantiarts.com

Cover image: Remy Gieling / unsplash.com

Photograph of author on page 223 was taken by
©Elias Wakan and used with his permission.

Printed in the United States of America

ISBN: 978-1-951651-55-8 (softcover)

Library of Congress Control Number: 2020948543

To Eli,
as always

CONTENTS

NOTES

Miscellaneous haiku and tanka appear in italics at the end of a few sections. Haiku and tanka with one space between them are part of a set. Haiku and tanka with two spaces between them should be read as separate poems. Often I have taken a haiku and later added two lines to it to make a tanka. The haiku must have lingered with me and demanded additions.

"ON READING ISSA EACH MORNING" first appeared as a Monday Poem by Leaf Press.

The poems in the section titled "SEGUES" were originally published by Wolsak and Wynn in a book of that name. The poems from "SEX AFTER 70," (Pacific-Rim Publishers) and "AND AFTER 80 . . . " (Pacific-Rim Publishers) also appeared in *Bent Arm for a Pillow* (Pacific-Rim Publishers, 2016).

The Poet Laureate poems all appeared in *Naomi in Nanaimo, Naomi in Nanaimo Again,* and *Naomi in Nanaimo at Last.*

PREFACE

While basically a personal essayist, I must admit that poetry
in the form of haiku, tanka, and free verse has occupied
a large percentage of my waking hours and many of my
sleeping ones. Frequently, I have woken with a poem ready
written, my subconscious having been working for me like a
fairy-tale gnome while I was resting.

My early poems, written in my late twenties and thirties,
seem very strange and distant to me now at eighty-nine.
Yet, on closer reading, they already are full of those endless
questions that have no answers that fill my later poems.

My couple of years living in Japan in the 1980s resulted in me
being caught in a net of haiku, tanka, and renku for the next
thirty years. It was a very willing capture, I must admit, for the
strong nouns of haiku grounded me in my sense organs and
the feelings and ideas that can be expressed in tanka allowed
me an outlet for my philosophical, if rather cynical, approach
to life. Renku, the game of linked verse poetry written together
by several poets, encouraged me to trust my intuition so I could
tune into the poet's words whose lines I would be picking up on
when my turn came around. Thus Japanese poetry forms were
the perfect vehicle for exploring Jung's four aspects of a human
being—sensing, feeling, thinking, and intuiting.

My free verse has allowed me a looser way to put into
words whatever it was I wanted to tell the world. Mostly,
this was a repetition of the fact that I found life bittersweet:
my daily existence being too wonderful to ever want
to leave it, but the occasional day occurring when I
considered the foolishness of mankind being totally

unbearable, resulting in me wanting to depart almost immediately.

I had the honor of being Poet Laureate of Nanaimo from 2014–16. Writing on demand for events happening in a small city made me realize how much a small town girl I was and how my writing matched so well the modest demands that a provincial city asked of me. Poetry writing made me a full human being, and producing poems for civic and island events allowed me to be able to pay back my island community of Gabriola and my friends in Nanaimo for the years they encouraged my writing and gave it an outlet.

Four of my books have been entirely devoted to poetry—*Segues, Sex After 70, And After 80 . . .* , and *Bent Arm for a Pillow*. Along with my early unpublished poems, I have selected the most reproduced of my poems from those books for the first part of *Wind on the Heath*. The last portion consists of new poems written between 2018 and 2020.

> Life is sweet brother . . .
> there's night and day brother,
> both sweet things;
> sun, moon and stars, brother,
> all sweet things;
> there's likewise a wind on the heath.
> Life is very sweet, brother;
> Who would wish to die?
> —George Borrow, *Lavengro*

Naomi Beth Wakan

EARLY POEMS

1966–75

VIRGIN IN A TREE

a drawing by Paul Klee

What price the juicy fruit now?
Where the luscious liquids
and sweet odors?
Where the full-blown curves
and ripest core?
The prize too long guarded
now skin-withered, pulp-wormed
pit-barren,
for want of plucking
all is dust dry.

WATCHERS

For what are we waiting
we watchers from balconies,
lingering long after
the children are bedward,
and the last bird and tree
have faded into the chocolate sky?
Why do we remain
peering out into the night?
Do we hope suddenly
to pierce the foolishness
of the world
by the intentness of our vision?
Seeking in the darkness
a crack through which
we may glimpse reality.

DOMESTIC PIECES

nearly haiku, written long before I knew the word "haiku"

on opening
the morning paper, I shed tears
for whom?

my name on the pill-box
is it I then who am
taking the pills?

kneidlach and tzimmes
is that the heritage I offer
my children?

studying so much
is there life that I am
leaving unlived?

ON WAKING AT THREE O'CLOCK IN THE MORNING

What is this keen awareness
I have at three o'clock in the morning?
Bed, shelf, mirror are estranged
and yet I move on the rim
of a significance.
All seems essentially clear
and yet in flux
so it evades my grasping words.
Perspectives shift,
outlines dissolve,
import vanishes.
The moment is as painful as
a memory just beyond recall.

WHAT ARE PEOPLE FOR?

Some I taste slowly,
nibbling around the edge,
closer and closer,
deliciously anticipating
the tasty center.
Others I swallow
at one gulp.
Coveting the sight
and feeling the weight later,
but missing the in-between
flavor.
Needing more,
needing less;
all the while wondering
if not for devouring,
what are people really for?

THE PUBLIC

See how the artist is acclaimed.
Triumphant he rides on their shoulders.
A little ridiculous, but yet aloft.
Whilst underneath their feet
is trampled last week's wonder.
In the middle the insatiable public.

BEVERLY RISES

Beverly rises,
her eyes swollen with dreams.
The lids falter,
reluctant to admit
the school-going morning

GRINNING

You enter me and I lie there grinning
with that innocent, simpleton smile
that welcomes everything.
I think of another time
when I had also lain there grinning
whilst the women around cursed
their husbands and God and anyone else
they felt responsible
for their agony.
And calling loudly for their mothers,
forgetting that soon they too
would have children calling out for them.
But I just lay there grinning.
And when they wheeled me in, I raised myself
on my elbows and saw
in the mirror at my feet
the head of my daughter emerging.
Then the grin broke into a cry
of wild joy, and I lay back exhausted,
as now, when I hold you reborn in my arms.

TOWELS

I stand at the cupboard
sorting towels.
On the right are the puffy bath towels,
and on the left "his," "hers," and "theirs"
hand towels and face cloths.
I am embarrassed to be counting towels
as if their counting could somehow
add to my essence.
I feel guilty I have towels in the cupboard,
and indeed, have a cupboard in which
to put towels.
I have an urge to gather them
and rush out to drop them in the arms
of people on the street.
How wide-eyed they would stand as
I thrust my burden onto them.
A gesture in futility.
So here I am stuck with my towels,
a toweled Pharisee ,
knowing that keeping them isn't enough,
yet not understanding how to give.

from

SEGUES
2005

ONE DOES NOT WRITE

One does not write
because the goldfish play
at the bottom of the waterfall,
but because not everyone
can see them.

HOW TO WRITE A HAIKU

Details confuse me,
so when I see a rose,
although I do not know
its pedigree, I write down "rose."
And when I cut it,
I do not know whether
I should cut it on a slant,
or straight, or under water twice,
so I write down "cut."
And when I put it in a vase,
I do not know whether it is raku
or glaze or, perhaps, good plastic,
so I write down "vase."
And when I see two red leaves
on the earth beside the rose bush,
I do not know from which tree
they have fallen,
so I write down "red leaves."
And as I set the vase
and the leaves on the table,
I write down

rose just cut
beside the vase
two red leaves

And although I do not know
the details of what I have just done,
the sadness of it all
cracks my heart open.

PADDLING ACROSS THE TABLECLOTH

A stranger leaves a strange piece
on my table, a portion of her life
she now feels ready to toss off,
to make a closure. And who better
to discard on than I, the collector
of others' dross and dead dreams.
It is a carved flat-bottom boat from Nigeria,
with two paddlers, three passengers,
and a mess of carved coconuts and cassava.
I am tempted to toss it in turn,
but am caught by the determined faces
of the oarsmen and by the stoicism
in the features of the others.
The baby, slung low on its mother's back,
doesn't utter a sound,
and the earthenware pot is empty.
On a whim, I cut giant sunflowers
and place them in a vase beside
this distant crew. The plants loom
over the boat—menacing yet protective
at the same time; a jungle river
reproduced on my tablecloth.
The evening shadows darken the scene.
In the morning, I see the boat has made
little, if any, progress across the tablecloth,
but the travelers have acquired a thick coating
of pollen on their hats and shoulders.

THE SCULPTOR

Ah! It is winter again
and you will disappear
into the basement of your being
for a month, or two.
When the first nettles
push the ground,
you'll slowly mount the stairs,
pale as a rabbinical student,
or a piece of forced endive,
bearing in your arms
a pristine sculpture.

A DREAMER OF SMALL DREAMS

Oh I am a dreamer of small dreams.
No house in Mayfair for me, nor
castle in Spain, or in Tuscany.
Are there castles in Tuscany?
Mine not to dream of heroes
on white horses (almost an anagram of heroes).
See there, I get distracted.
Distracted by the beans pushing
through—I dream of them
climbing the poles I have set ready.
And the new pea sprouts—I dream
they will cover the wire fence.
I dream of my brushes that will
paint a really good green pepper,
and I dream of my dreams that
they might give forth a fine
line for a poem every day.
Oh I am a dreamer of small dreams
on my island of no significance.

SEX AFTER 70

I sit across
from my publisher
who cuddles his coffee
and explodes with "What!"
"I'm writing a book on haiku,"
I repeat calmly.
"On haiku!" his face red.
"Why can't you write
something people want to read
like *Fishing on the West Coast?*"
"Or *Sex after 70?*" I counter.
"Yes, *Sex after 70,*"
his eyes switch from
exasperated to hopeful.
"Now there's a promising title!"
We both fall silent.
I imagine he is weighing up
the odds of me being informed
on the subject, while I
do a quick survey of
a possible table of contents.
Sex and osteoarthritis—
the joints locking
in positions unheard of
in the Kama sutra.
Choices—orgasm or muscle cramp;
whether to allow myself
the pleasure of orgasm
or go into the pain
of a concurrent foot cramp.

Whether to focus on the vagina
and the blissful dissolving,
or on the foot and get that spasm
dealt with and those
toes straightened out.
Decisions, decisions and
before I know it I am
thinking of nouns—
those nouns of haiku,
and how each noun
condenses a universe
and packs a wallop,
and how two or three nouns
together, if carefully chosen,
can tumble you into the void
and to Universes beyond,
and how the pause, the pause
at the 5th or 12th syllable,
opens so many possibilities
to dwarf all orgasms, or cramps
come to that, and transforms
dark crows on bare branches
into cockatoos on plum blossoms.
"I'm writing the book on haiku,"
I firmly address my publisher
across the steam of his coffee.
He sighs, takes a sip and asks,
"When's the first draft ready?"

CANCER EPISODE

news of shadows—
the secretary calls
to casually report

first sun—
baring suspect breasts
in Drumbeg Park

early sunlight—
I rub hot stones on
my breasts

a charm hanging
over the phone, hoping for
good results.

cancer support group—
next to the tea and cookies
a plastic breast

two surgeons
gossip; washing up to
their elbows

awake
during surgery, I control
my swearing

my surgeon
talks of his four boys;
the smoke rises

recovery room—
two nurses fight over
my gurney

photographing
each stage for the reluctant
surgeon

confession
the margins aren't clear . . .
mutual forgiveness

drawing out the tube
a ripple passes across
my chest

reaching
to her breast scar, he cups
his hand

sculptor and surgeon
discuss the remodeling
of my breast

two free bras
and a prosthesis! What
a rich country!

REFLECTIONS WHILE LOVEMAKING

I lie and watch the snowflakes
descending on the skylight as
he explores my body. I give
an occasional sigh or moan
lest he think I am not completely
with him, but most of me
is pondering on the perfect symmetry
of each flake as it falls, and
as he enters me, I switch to wonder
at the chaos of the flakes
as they become a thin sheet
of mush on the glass. I seek
for patterns in their randomness.
As we rise together in our own
peculiar symmetry, I consider
the thermodynamics that allows
the flakes to pile up more at the top end
of the skylight, and while
he groans with contentment, I
muse on the ethics of multi-tasking.

LOVING IN SIMPLE WAYS

Love low-income style
appears in different guises.
Skimming the library web,
he orders new books
that might interest her,
so they are ready piled
on the OUT desk when she visits.
And on a walk to the shore,
he pauses to pick up a stone,
a leaf, a shell that has attracted
his attention, and that he hopes
will enchant her too.
Night time, he lifts the covers
welcoming her to his warmth.
And she, too, welcomes him back;
back from the separate places
they had retreated to for dealing
with the abrasions of the day.

from

SEX AFTER 70
2010

AT NIGHT

At night she strides
across the plateau
of her dreams
with legs up to there,
buttocks raised, and arms
awash with silver.
Daytime she loads
the washer and hugs
herself from time to time,
keeping the organs in place
and hoping wistfully
for just one more year.

THE LAST CLEAR MORNING OF MY LIFE

The last clear morning of my life,
we startled a young buck; his antlers,
newly grown, just showed above his ears.
The last clear morning of my life,
the bald eagle circled the water and
tried time and time again to claw a fish.
The last clear morning of my life, we watched
an otter preen himself on an early sun-hot rock.
Pretending to be trees, we drew very close.
His mate appeared from the water
and asked him to check on those "trees,"
as our cameras clicked across the morning.
"Just as I expected!" she said.
And, wiggling their bottoms to shit in disdain,
they slid into the tide.
All this on the last clear morning
of my life.

RECYCLING TIME

From spiritual greed
I seized all ceremonies offered
and hung my neck and wrists
with an assortment of charms
and amulets and empowerments
that would make a devotee blush,
and made my mother so embarrassed
that she refused to introduce me
to the bank manager's wife when
she paid a social visit.
One day, when a candle was put out
on my third eye (or perhaps when
I drank from a human skull in Sikkim,
or floated lanterns in a foreign bay),
in greed I took the Boddhisattva vow
and found I had promised eagerly,
but unwisely, to return to Earth
after my death, time and time again
until I had saved all sentient beings,
or brought them to Buddha,
or dragged them from the Devil
(or some such arrangement).
Now older, though little wiser,
with greed hanging limp as my breasts,
I would, if it was in my power,
order most sentient beings
immediately recycled (myself included)
and cancel all vows made in confusion.

BREASTS

I heard a story once
(I can no longer remember where)
of a young man becoming
entranced by an older woman
("Nothing new there," you'll say
... but wait).
She was an artist, and
day after day he watched
the movement of her arm,
her wrist, her hand,
and day after day
he listened to her speak
of colors and canvas ...
she could speak of cocoa
and he would have watched
closely as her lips
formed the word.
One evening her lips
said the following:
"I know you would like
to bed with me, and
I would like that too,
but first I must
tell you something."
He nods ... "Anything, anything."
"I have had a double mastectomy."
His face wrinkles in puzzlement.
"I have no breasts," she states.
He pauses, then quickly
is through the gate and away.

I too have a story
of a younger man who watches.
He watches as my breast
is chipped away, bit by bit.
He watches as it finally disappears;
watches as the bandages come off;
watches as the drainage tube
snakes across my chest;
watches as the scar fades.
And he celebrates his Amazon,
who is both maid and crone,
and gently rubs cream
onto the flattened place.
He does not need to tell me
"It makes no difference."
We both know now the sweetness
that it does and it doesn't.

MOM AND DAD

In my writing workshops I ask my students to re-parent themselves with literary role models. For my own choice as poetry parents, I chose Billy Collins and Wisława Szymborska, though I have some doubts about their domestic capabilities.

Oh! if only Billy
had been my father
and Wisława my mother,
how my poetry would have shone,
and my small hand been encouraged
to move over the page.
Standing barefoot on
the lawn with Billy
in the dew-filled morning,
how my little voice
would have lisped out
rhymes about the budding cherry tree,
and in the evening,
Wisława would have filled
my small head with legends
from the polka past
and ideas that went beyond
right and wrong. I suspect,
however, the meals would have
been a little slap-dash,
and when I might have
wanted Billy, he would not
have been there . . .
even if he was.

A HAIJIN'S LIFE

haiku? senryu?
who cares so long as the heart
pauses in mid-beat

haijin discuss
whether the essence of haiku
is "suchness"
mosquitoes, this summer evening,
buzz around the deck.

cleaning house
after the haiku meet . . .
one poem lingers

no paper
I write a haiku
on a shell

when on the way
to the mail, fearful
of a rejection envelope,
an owl flies low across my path,
all cares of "Yes" or "No" vanish

at the bank
the teller discusses
lay-offs
I'm secure in the thought
"I live by my poetry"

ON READING

when reading
I search for meaning
between the words
in the spaces at ends of chapters
somewhere in the index

when reading
even in fiction I search
for "how to"
how to live more fully
how to bite into an autumn fruit

when reading
a book of tanka
I'm surprised
at how many ways there are
to say "I'm lonely"

reading on the deck
my list of "things to do"
as a book mark

I'M NOT MARGARET ATWOOD

"I'm not Margaret Atwood"
I assure them earnestly,
meaning I am small of talent
and the same of fame.
I do, however, have curly hair
and am also the mother of a daughter.
Once, some years ago, we,
that is Margaret Atwood and I,
both applied for jobs at Bell Telephone.
Margaret was rejected, being
over-burdened with an M.A.
I, with my simple B.Com. was accepted,
although my language, they indicated,
was a little odd. And why not, since I had
just disembarked from the immigrant ship,
Samaria, the week before and had
yet to add "Eh" to my verbal punctuation.
I didn't take the job, but moved
to Market Research, where, apparently,
Margaret too found work and, at
some other point, we both back-to-the-landed,
although Margaret's domestic animals
far exceeded my pathetic brood of bantams.
I've probably written more books than she has,
although each had 1/10th of the pages
and 1/1000 of the sales . . . but still,
if Margaret Atwood had had
a very much smaller sister,
smaller in every way,
I might have been mistaken for her
by some provincial critic.

APPLESAUCE POETRY

Why am I cooking applesauce
from the first culls of our trees
when I could be writing a great poem,
or at least, a good one?
Perhaps a poem hitting hard
at mankind's weak spots—
always the easiest to attack,
or a poem to soften the edges
of sorrow, as if a poem
could ever do that.
Instead of which, I am
cutting the wormed places out
and chopping the small,
green apples, skin and all.
Then I am throwing them
into some bubbling water and
letting them boil until
the froth bursts everything open.
The froth, thick as mashed potatoes,
is sieved of its peel and its cores,
and touched with cinnamon and honey.
Ah! If only I could write
a poem about that.

MY SMALL SQUARE

My life is like a small square
that I choose to live within.
Outside is no more evil
than inside, for, being
human, all qualities, good
or bad, are to be found in
this skin/flesh/bone bag of nonsense;
albeit drawn modest.
Inside my boundaries,
I write of spiders scattering
from a clothespin bag and
the unsuspected autumn crocus
purpling the ground—
petty things, yet, within
my small square, they
fill to the corners.

OUR CLAY

based on the lines by Kuan Tao-Sheng:
"I am in your clay / You are in my clay"

Am I in your clay
and you in mine?
I've never thought
of these thirty years
that way; not even once.
I've thought of making
good meals and a comfy home;
flowers from the garden
for the table, a good poem
occasionally, and royalties
to pay the mortgage.

Am I in your clay
and you in mine?
The question makes me uncomfy.
It's too exaggerated for
my English conditioning,
too demanding for something
I had taken for granted.
Still it won't go away,
so I start to count more carefully
the five to ten fruit and veg
I prepare each day,
read the odd book you recommend,
and self-consciously wash
the sheets more frequently.
I have sex a little more than I want,
and plump the pillows every morning.

Am I in your clay
and you in mine?
Still the question remains
unanswered between us.
Besides the added zest
I am trying to add to each element
of our partnership
is now attached guilt and shame
and embarrassment at my
somewhat less than perfect love.

Am I in your clay
and you in mine?
The quote has become a koan,
so one dawn I wake
in a fever of failure.
I note you are lying against me,
hand on my breast,
and I have a determined
arm around your shoulders.
Then, in an instant,
I know not how, all dissolves
and I ask myself in confusion,
Whose hand? Whose breast?
Whose arm? Whose shoulders?
And the tears run down over my clay
and your clay, your clay
and mine.

REPRIMAND TO THOSE JAPANESE COURT WOMEN

The Heian women whom I am addressing in this poem
can be found in Murasaki Shikibu's *Genji Monogatari*
and in the women's diaries from that period.

Italics are allusions to list titles from
Sei Shōnagon's *The Pillow Book*.

Oh you stupid court women!
Have you nothing better to do
than spend long nights crying
into your futon about how
you can still feel his hands
in your disheveled hair,
still smell the lingering scent
of his clothes on your own.
Why, anything triggers your tears:
the call of a mountain cuckoo,
the quail crying out,
or the plover piping.
Your buckwheat pillow is soggy
and your koto is out of tune.
Can't you see the paths
to your house are overgrown
and deep in snow?
You must understand that the gods
have decreed your northwesterly
direction forbidden to him
for the rest of the year,
and probably the rest of your life!

Your heart may be withering,
the skies filled with clouds,
and even the moon is slow and sinking,
yet gazing at your soaked pillow,
and trying to unknot your twisted strands
will not help matters at all.
Why don't you read Sei Shōnagon
and take matters into your own hands.
Start making lists. That will stop
the flow of your tears.
Begin with *Depressing Things*
and get them out of your system.
Next, *Things That Should Be Short*,
such as unrequited love.
Soon you'll be brushing your long hair
and grinding a load of fresh ink
in order to list
Things That Have Lost Their Power.

NOTES FOR MEASUREMENT OF A BED

Wide enough for sulking,
but not too wide for making-up;
soft enough to retain
the imprint of love,
but hard enough to etch in
the shadows of loneliness,
that seem twice as black
within the intimacy.
Pillows should be stuffed
with secret pillow talk
and slightly dampened from unshed tears.
The coverlet should be a patchwork
of the ups and downs of two people
living mostly in union.
Sheets should be washed each week
in a lather of forgiveness,
and returned to the bed
fresh with hope.

harlequin couple
paddling out into the bay
their wakes intersecting

trees, mist, mountains
trees, mist, mountains
west coast morning

first harlequin she's seen
she hugs everyone in sight
even strangers

on the December beach
not a sign to be seen
of Christmas

heavy snowfall
silent, so silent,
even the fridge

first washing on the line
reaching in the clothespin bag
spiders scatter

cutting her neighbor's
branch of cherry blossom, she prays
for forgiveness

ON READING ISSA EACH MORNING

Every morning,
as others open their papers
to the sports page, or
keep them closed on
the grim rumors of the day,
I receive a small, sweet message
by e-mail; a message
telling of simple things . . .
midday naps, the scent of the lotus,
deer rutting, and mountain rain,
a sickle moon, a temple bell,
muddy straw sandals, the beggar's stove,
first frost, and slush-splashed robes,
plum blossom, Buddharupas,
saké cups, radishes,
garbage-removers, mosquitoes
at the eaves, and a cottage door
crushed by morning glories,
tumbled down houses, and dogs
mouthing down rice cakes.
Only occasionally a bigger mystery
presents itself for my morning
consideration, such as
a samurai's discarded top knot.

BARK-MULCH PATHS

Before I knew
where they would lead,
I laid the paths of our garden.
The rain-soaked bark-mulch
gave a clear outline
to possibilities
and potential beds.
My pathways offered structure
in the wilderness of untamed grasses
that swept our septic field,
and showed the inroads
we would need to take
before we could settle comfortably
our bargain with the wild.

KIP AT NEW MOON IN AUGUST

when the dinoflagellates sparkle in disturbed waters

Flashes of light
from the parking lot,
then flashes down the trail
to where we sit in the dark.
A family of six or so approach.
Much giggling as
clothes are flung off
and toes touch the cool waters.
Then splash!
And the water is full
of sparkling angels
and we gasp once more at
the beauty of August waters
at new moon.
Kip stands ready to dive,
admiring for a moment
his shiny flock.
"How much we have
to be thankful for
on this magic island
of ours," he calls
out to the stars.
And somehow the simple words
become hallowed
as he plunges in, to be
transformed to an angel himself.

AUTUMN

That season of paradox
when plenitude lies
on the kitchen table,
ready for cellar and canning
and the drying trays;
when garlic hangs braided
from the beams and
herbs shrivel above the stove.
Yet, at the same time,
cobwebs hint of graves opening
and the ghosts of All Hallow's Eve beckon,
so that each fruit lying ready,
though in its prime, seems touched
with a hint of decay, and
sad leaves scatter the flower beds.

GAMAN

after reading about the internment
camps for Japanese during WWII;
Gaman: bearing the unbearable with dignity

And in the tar-paper shacks,
with no tools at hand,
they forged chisels from bed-springs,
knives from abandoned animal traps,
and made string from old onions sacks.
And with these, they shaped the impossible—
teapots from hard rock,
baskets from scrap papers.
They even made paintings on
their evacuation notices themselves.
They taught their children to write
using chimney soot for ink,
and to type using letters cut circular
from old Eaton's catalogues.
Their bitterness melted down
to make community,
their resignation sparked
into creativity—an insult
transmuted into art.
When humanity goes crazy
and fear overtakes reason,
it's folks with *gaman*
who laugh with lizards
and walk straight-backed
into the mists.

KEEPING CLOTHES WHITE

Everyone has something they do
when there is nothing else
that can be done—some knit,
some jog, some pour
alcohol down their throats,
and then . . .
some choose to do the laundry.

The summer of our separation
I washed white trousers,
white socks, white shirts,
white shorts, as if my marriage
depended on their whiteness.
So when I heard of the woman
living in the Gaza strip
going to the pump for water and
searching for bits of soap
to keep the girls' dresses white,
I recognized a sister straightaway.
For though we were oceans apart,
that summer we could have been
standing side by side together
pumping water to keep our
children's clothes white.
Not knowing, in our desperation,
what other action could be taken.

AMBITION

To reach an age when things
fall away unneeded,
as spent petals on a flower,
as fall leaves from the tree,
as skins of summer snakes.
When Socrates passed the market stalls
he noted, "What a lot
of things I don't need."
Ah! that's what I mean.

BEACH GLASS

Will someone take me aside now?
                    Now that the tides have
                    thrown me on beaches
                    and drawn me under
                    times beyond count.
                    Now that the waters
                    have tumbled me
                    this way and that,
                    so the sandstone
                    has blunted all
                    sharp edges and
                    I curl within,
                    my boundaries softened.
Will someone take me aside now
thinking me worth considering
from time to time?

I'M A MOMENT

I'm a moment.
A pile of dust
with a point of view.
My ideas? They come
from a command post
far from consciousness.
My feelings, chameleon-like,
change as the breezes,
one thousand times a day;
at the slightest nudge,
offence, favor.
There is no substance
to such a being . . .
I'm just a shifting
with opinions,
a trembling
of trivialities,
yet somehow essential.

SYMMETRY

Oh, if only my eyes
had been further apart,
and my nose
a little less prominent,
and the length from
my knees to my heels
three inches more
to match my excellent thighs,
I could have snagged
a baron in his castle,
or a count in his aerie chalet,
or a Hollywood mogul's
26-bedroom cottage.
But my body is as it is
and all the above
never happened.
And so I live in a small
vinyl-sided cottage
on a tiny island.
I am attached to
a many-years-my-junior man
who occasionally looks
like Robert Redford, and
who, when he is not
musing on his next sculpture,
is dwelling on his two strawberry patches
and whether the birds will
get the cherries.
So really, I have little
to whine about, even though
my eyes are too close.

serving at the funeral
how greedily the survivors
fill their plates . . .
a man uses a crust to wipe
the last remains away

this lifetime
of so many moves that when
I have a longing
to go home, I can no longer
recall where it would be

heavy rain
in the puddle the skeleton
of a Chinese lantern

a heron
strikes at its reflection
shallow water
still, I wonder if I'm
in too deep

the little monk
steps into the void
laughing

NEARLY WATERFRONT

I have hated
but never with a knife in my hand.
Loved, but rarely dissolved
skin between us.
Cried, but only
from the tear ducts.
Despaired, but never near
railway tracks or waterways.
I have been to Hiroshima,
but didn't enter.

The story of my life—
nearly waterfront

THINGS I LOVE TO SEE IN THE EARLY MORNING

The king of eagles
bald-headed on
his allotted tree;
the snow-covered mountains
Onley-like, mist lifting
to reveal them;
lady's slippers
peering up from the salal;
rows of my lettuce
in parallel formation
heavy with dew;
my lover's tender
absent-minded smile
when I ask him
about domestic chores
that need doing
that day.

TO OZU

the Japanese film director

On his gravestone
in Chinese letters
is written
"nothingness"
for that is what he sought
through all his films . . .
that void where good
slips over bad, and
"yes" and "no" are stamped
on the same coin, and
edges fade perhaps into
Rumi's field beyond.
And Ozu sought that void
not in exotic places,
or with esoteric clothes,
or with oil anointed
on his head, but
through everyday acts
where forlornness looms large—
births, marriages, and deaths,
and everywhere
loneliness, loneliness, loneliness,
where skin divides
and even your face in the mirror
will not reply to your
endless questions, and
your shadow, when approached,
turns slightly away.

THINGS I LEARNED IN CHILDHOOD

I learned— bacon was evil;
            shell-fish gave you typhoid;
            mushrooms were excessive
            to most family budgets,
            but especially ours;
            Jesus never meant to hurt the Jews
            since he was one himself;
            Wagner should never be listened to;
            "Hitler" was a forbidden word;
            and that I was special.

I learned— tap-dancing was vulgar
            and somehow threatening;
            child-beauty competitions
            were for other children;
            and stuff I wanted to know about
            was in a little book
            hidden on the top shelf
            of the cupboard which stored
            my mother's muskrat coat;
            I learned my father's body was good
            although I wasn't allowed
            to check this out;
            and that I was special.

I learned— children went hungry in Europe
and men died in Europe
for reasons that they, or
someone else, thought were good;
that it makes you feel warm
when you give stuff you don't want
to poor people and that
they should be grateful;
that rich and poor were because
governments were bad;
but that as dad was a civil servant,
governments were also good;
and . . . I almost forgot . . .
that I was special.

JIM THOMPSON'S SILK HOUSE, BANGKOK

How well he understood
that when you put on silk
you irridesce as tropical beetles,
your heart eases, your body youthens,
and all is caresses.
So what he disappeared into the Highlands!
Why do they dwell on that?
We all must disappear, Highlands
or Lowlands, though it's true
our passing may lack the rumored
drama of CIA or wild beasts.
Better to stay with the drama of his silk
and the six houses he gathered
together to make into one home.
Now, in that house, money flows
as tourists, surrendering totally,
buy yards of his shining silk.
The blues, the golds, the greens . . .
one feels faint in that house,
and searches for a chair in vain,
for all there is from floor to rafters
are bolts of shimmering silk
and the sound of the prayer call
from across the Baan Krua Kh long,
from where his Moslem weavers
first came those long silk years ago.

THE LITTLE BOY DANCES

At the community barbecue
the children dance
on the grass in front of the stage.
The girls strut around
wriggling their tiny bodies
like strippers drawn small;
even the two-year-olds
are making like sexy.
But in their midst
a solitary boy dances.
He stamps in time
with the rhythms,
flinging his arms,
this way and that.
Then, finding a pattern
with his legs that he likes,
repeats it for a while.
He is unaware of the 700 or so
of us sitting on our chairs watching him
while chomping on wild salmon
and canned beans and pickled beets
and potato salad and
watermelon chunks, and
I am suddenly so fearful
of what the world will offer
this wondrous small boy; his feet
demanding the soil and
his arms enfolding the sky
at the island salmon barbecue.

FÜR ELISE

I am seated playing
Für Elise from sheet music
that I have rescued
from the recycling bin.
The pages are covered
with nota benes—
places where the student
has fumbled and stumbled,
and I wonder for whom
they were written.
I picture a young girl
seated at an ancient upright.
She flinches slightly when
she misses an accidental
and holds her breath
while playing the arpeggios
to make them extra smooth.
Her right foot, clad
in white stocking and
patent leather shoe,
steadily pumps the pedals,
and her young breasts
heave and sigh with
the crescendos and
diminuendos.
And oh! Her tranquil face,
her lake-blue eyes,
her every-night-brushed hair
make me hope that she mastered
the nota benes quickly, and
went on to better things.

cold wind on the beach
memories of school uniforms
always too big

away from his child
he takes his afternoon nap
on our sofa

nightfall
a small boat comes into the bay
dropping anchor . . .
echoes from our many journeys
reach us on the dock

staccato staples
and the remnants of
important notices . . .
have I told you recently
that I love you?

reflections
of anchored small boats ripple
in the lake
I too feel fragmented
when I think of past ventures.

pondering impermanence
to the sound of logging
on the lot next door

MOVE FORWARD

When the sun breaks
the morning leaves apart,
I know the peas will pod,
the scarlet-runners will flower,
children will flourish, and
that some creative being
is working full steam ahead.
All is intelligence.

When the rain threatens the skylights
and my limbs are reluctant to move,
I suspect the broccoli will never make it,
know the kiwis are the wrong sex,
and that every action is doubtful,
and wonder at the stupidity
of whoever started it all and
wish it was over.

When the wind blows the septic field
grasses every which way,
I think that what you say is the truth,
and also what she, and what he, says.
I would also believe what I said
if I knew what I was saying.
At such time, I believe the creator
of it all is tacking frantically
this way, then that.

When the fog descends like a shroud
on our vinyl-sided cottage and
the ships' horns blow in the channel,
and the captain cannot see his nose
in front of him, and the robins
circle over the bird bath,
then I know nothing, except that
even though there is no clear view
and that the creator is dubious,
yet still we must move forward blindly.

PIN TUCKS

I look at the lattice
of pin tucks that
Vionnet has created,
coming down from
the left-side
and the right-side
and interweaving between
the stomach and groin
in a mystery of tiny stitches.
And, knowing this garment
is for snagging a rich man,
and knowing the gap
between a woman
who could buy such a dress
and a woman covered in rags
snatched from a barrio heap
will spell the death
of my planet . . .
yet still I wonder
at Vionnet's cunning,
and the skill of
the seamstress . . . and
what it might feel like
to one day wear
such a miracle myself.

PRETENDING

I am sitting in a hot bath,
when, from nowhere, I say to him
"One of us will die first."
"Yes," he replied, "I was
thinking just that as I read
of the death of Darwin's daughter.
I wanted to rush out into
the garden and give you a kiss,
but I thought you would be having
a good time and didn't want
to disturb you."
"Yes, I was," I reply.
"I was pruning away like
someone possessed and feeling
like it was a purification.
I would have hated to think
about death at that moment.
I wasn't ready." I add
"I don't want us to die."
He leans over the bath to kiss
my upturned face and we both smile.
We know it is inevitable
and that we are just foolish
children pretending for a moment
that it will never happen.

from

AND AFTER 80…
2013

CHERRY BLOSSOM HAIKU

spring thaw—
the trees with an aura
of promised cherries

yet one more haiku
on cherry blossom. Are there
really new things to say?

faces raised
to the just-opened blossoms
mouths shaped in an "Ah!"

a blanket spread
under the cherry blossoms
teens work their iPhones

a sudden gust
and blossoms just on the trees
are just on the ground

fresh blossoms
yet everything feels
exactly the same

outside the food bank
the row of cherry trees
feeds the eyes

WINTER

The sound of no sound . . .
as fallen trees down power lines
so even the fridge cannot be heard.
The sound of no sound . . .
just small holes appearing in the snow
as icicles melt from gutters.
The sound of no sound . . .
just scarlet berries left on the mountain ash
and the spiralings of curly willow branches.

RELATIONSHIPS

his matching towel
no longer hanging
next to hers

wedding anniversary
sixtieth? sixty-fifth?
they can't remember

lost love . . .
how well we know
in January
what we shouldn't have said
in December

though together,
we each must travel solo . . .
just a glimpse
from time to time across
a lonely mountain valley

sharing our foreign coins
at the airport for a last
few snacks . . .
passing travelers then,
yet still together years later

Valentine's day
is it massacre or love?
sometimes
it's hard to tell the difference . . .
he says he has no regrets

10 TANKA FOR KRISHNAMURTI

The lines in italics are borrowed from Krishnamurti.

children
building a rocket-ship
with cardboard boxes
angels may fear to tread, but ah
the confidence of innocence

holding
her grandchild's hand
outside the zoo
she suddenly feels happy . . .
and lingers in the moment

lifting the rock
children shriek with delight
as hidden crabs scatter
the ringing of bells and eating of wafer
has nothing to do with searching

he looks closely
at a small wasps' nest
built in a cavity . . .
without awareness of things
most people are as good as dead

knowing the planet
is round is helpful for
truth-seekers
beginning here will return you here
there is no end to the journey

no matter
how many words we say
to each other
the essence lies in the spaces between
the essence lies in the pauses

why search
for gurus in haystacks
cleaning out your ears
alert to what they are saying?
it is you who has to understand life

wanting this
or that to happen
is futile
everything is set in jelly
ambitions breed anxiety

going to
the ends of the earth
is a waste of energy
hang around the homestead for
truth may be under a dead leaf

they watch admiringly
as the father quail supervises
his noisy offspring
while mother pecks at the clover
is not life an extraordinary thing?

ENOUGH

"Once is enough,"
the abbot commented dryly
on hearing the novices
cracking their morning eggs.
Indeed, once is enough—
one birth, one death,
one vow to honor and obey,
one change of heart.
Once is—
one spring of cherry blossom,
one good fall of pumpkin,
one look into another's eyes,
one scanning of the horizon,
one holding of a small child,
one leaning over a sick bed.
One intense doing . . . of anything,
informs us of our being here,
and the possibility of us being
elsewhere also.

early sunlight
the gulls etch their shadows
on the cliff face

first wind of autumn
new school clothes always
too long

wind up from the beach
the campsite deserted save
a child's flip-flop sandal

autumn moon
our shadows walk together
old friends

July 1st
others celebrate
Canada Day
but I, ever ornery, give thanks
for there's quail in the meadow

COUPLE ON THE CAKE

"You are not making eye-contact,"
  the bride complains.
"Nor you, but still I am content
  here with your gown brushing
  the crease of my tux and
  your veil just flicking my ear."
"We are not going anywhere,"
  she tries again.
"Where is there to go
  when I am with you?"
"That's all very well,"
  her voice is strained,
"but we're not doing anything!"
"Not yet," he replies briefly.
"I feel so stuck," she almost whines.
"Why not?" he responds cheerfully.
"We are joined by a plastic piece
  and are up to our ankles in icing."
  She stares straight ahead.
  Her lips tighten into a smile
  and a stray piece of icing
  melts in the corner of one eye.

ISLAND RECITAL

island recital
I know almost everyone
in the audience

Rameau variations
on the island Steinway—my neighbor
claps in the wrong places

as the variations
reach their climax, three eagles
fly past the window

in the dolce variations
even in this small audience . . .
a candy unwrapper

fingers in the shadows
still find the right notes
on the piano

after the recital
a darkened room
and voices from the buffet

FOUR TANKA ON "HAIKU"

I have stood
in Bashō's birthplace
in Iga Ueno
longing for some inspiration
to rise from the dirt floor

I have just read
of Bashō's wife
(albeit common-law)
why in his thousands of haiku
did he not once tell of his love?

Shiki
a breath of fresh air
for haiku
a breath of fresh air
for Shiki

being
one himself
how could Issa
not be one with all underdogs . . .
the authenticity of his words

aficionados
listen to haiku and
sigh appropriately

whether bird or bird shit
the haijin seizes her pen
and writes a haiku

our new window seat
made for reading fiction
or distraught letters

my small voice
struggles its way
onto the page
hard to hear it when each moment
trawls with it past memories

safe houses
are needed in this world
guarded places—
caves, berry patches
and the shieldings of small poems

virgin poets launch
themselves loudly and lengthily
on open stage
we old hands follow with
our small but perfect mutterings

THE USES OF TANKA

In Heian times,
tanka were sweet confirmations
between courtier lovers
of deeds done and to be done.
And also of court rapists,
for dark chambers and
many-layers of kimono
hid identities, so seducers
were never quite sure that
they had entered the right woman.
Even in such cases of mistake,
the next morning the maiden
would receive a token tanka
speaking of her long hair perhaps,
and other matters, and it would be
attached to the prescribed branch
from say a flowering cherry.
She, in return, whether mad with anger,
sulking, or perhaps with a small smile,
would be obliged to also write a tanka
in response, commenting on the situation,
and send it along with maybe
a late-blooming plum blossom.
A few years later, both women,
whether seduced, or once loved,
might be found writing more acerbic tanka,
complaining of neglect, or at least
that the dwelling he had provided
for them was not up to par.
Tanka-writing would also be called for
when noblemen, at time of banishment,

(maybe for a political misstep, or
for the seduction of the Emperor's favorite)
thought sadly of the Capitol
they would be leaving for say
the beaches of Suma (always a good place
for writing mournful tanka of exile).
These days, I write tanka
when my haiku get uppity
with the conceit that they have
nailed the moment to the page.
I slap them with two extra lines,
reminding them that all things pass,
particularly the "here and now"
and even if things don't pass
as quickly as we would like,
it's all illusory anyway.
Yes, tanka are useful for times
such as these.

the story of my life
once more I get
honorable mention

do people who wish
me well, really do so?
reading too many
spy stories there's conspiracy
in the fridge, and even in the oven

yet one more
self-help book . . .
another trip
around myself, another trip
skirting the edge

spring cleaning . . .
I rearrange the dross
of yesterday
hoping it will prove adequate
for the path I'm on today

evening blinds
move gently with the breeze
casting shadows . . .
how dramatic I have made my life
out of the shallowest of incidents

longing always
for a home, that even
when I now have one,
I still feel myself with
a residual longing

I need a pill
for living, I don't ask much,
I don't need
an endless summer, just another
dimension to slip into occasionally

this life
is full of dangers
and difficulties
I pause a moment too long
before crossing the road

these last years
all ambitions have vanished
from my vocabulary
it's easier to be happy in a valley
than on a mountain top

THE START OF MODERN ART

And Kandinsky came in
from the meadow one day
and, glancing at his easel,
shifted uneasily,
not quite knowing why.
It was at that moment
that modern art was born,
for on his canvas,
no meadows, no grasses,
no bushes, no trees . . .
only colors and shapes
on his upside-down-placed canvas
and, if he had been
a flashy artist,
he would have jumped in the air
and turned somersaults.
But being severe and sober,
he merely coughed slightly
and smiled in a bemused way,
realizing that somehow he had
freed art from its subject,
by accident as it were;
shifted art towards music
by a mistake, and,
as he stared in wonder,
the bells rang out loud
from his canvas.

A SET OF BEDSIDE TANKA

on a full-moon night
I toss within a formless dream
seeking answers . . .
it is as wearisome as
trying to find prime factors

our bedroom
reflected in the standing mirror
how still and calm
no tales of angry words or
passionate forgiveness in the glass

a bed should be
wide enough for sulking
but not too wide
for making up and retaining
the imprint of love

early morning light
and skin touching skin . . .
no desire
just the warmth of contact
and the breeze moving the curtains

each morning
before I leave bed, I prepare
a list of things to do . . .
the day, willfully, takes off
in another direction

SOMETIMES I ADMIT

Sometimes I admit
to switching stations from
Mahler and Scriabin
and discordant new music
to Dolly's comforting voice
and the beat of a country song
that always finishes on
a perfect cadence.

Sometimes I admit to
putting down the latest
Booker prize-winner
with a sigh and taking up
a fast unliterate crime mystery,
or better yet, a spy story
telling of how the world
is really run by mad men.

Sometimes I admit that
keeping up with the latest
art theory is tiring and as
I can't even distinguish
postmodernism from premodernism
I often turn to calmly breathing in
a comforting pastoral landscape,
or a Ryder painting of men at sea
in a small boat, or I might dwell
for a time on the loneliness
of a Hopper restaurant.

Sometimes I admit
to tiring of reading of
saints and gurus whose
example it might be worth
following, and turn instead
to see how the Pitt-Jolie
relationship is turning out
and whether Cruz is still
married to Bardem.

Sometimes I admit to
checking out my horoscope
to estimate the odds
of my being taken seriously
by someone this lifetime.

"ON WAKING" TANKA

on waking
in a shower of rain
my limbs
sink into the mattress
as if half-immersed in clay

on waking
on a sunny morning
my body
light as a rolling tumbleweed
springs eagerly towards the day

on waking
on a frosty morning
my mind
a stretched piece of glass through which
all can be seen clearly

on waking
in a snowfall
the whiteness
brings a new light into the bedroom
radiant, yet silent

on waking
this morning
I'm a little out of focus
as if the world has got away from me . . .
has gone its own way

INHERITANCE

I inherited
my mother's unlived life
and feeling
her pressure to learn;
to not get pregnant
(at least not before marriage);
and then to marry well;
to exceed my middle-class roots;
to exceed the neighbors' children;
to exceed . . .
on leaving home
I reversed gear
on her ambitions
and became a wanderer.
Unless we guard well,
we will become
what our mothers want
what our fathers think best,
what our teachers value,
what our bosses expect,
what our partners phantasy,
what will keep our children's love.
Even at the moment
of death, still unaware of
what we truly need, we cry out
to those surrounding us,
"How do you want me to do this?"

waking
with a new poem
under my tongue
I lie in bed smiling, as if
the world were totally benign

at the reading
poets elbow each other hoping
to go on first
how far away a good poem seems
from the ambitious poet

there's no hurt,
no anger, no paranoia that
can't be cocooned
within a little poem;
its lethality subdued

even though doubtful
of life after death
somehow I sense that
because I write poetry
I'm destined for the Pure Land

THE SECRET CELL

I've come across a secret cell,
a pocket of anachronism,
a den of fans of past poets,
where rhyme and rhythm
are not forgotten—
yet whispered guardedly.
The members speak of
qualities that used to be
capitalized—
Valor, Virtue, Innocence,
Beauty, Nobility, Backbone,
yet with a certain hesitation,
as if unsure of their reality.
Wordsworth is recalled,
and Swinburne, Davies
and Kipling and Tennyson;
names faded from current
academic classes for
their possible incorrectness
in all political ways.
Ah! You group of anarchists
paging through your treasuries,
is it just nostalgia for times long ago
that you gather,
or could it be an urgent
conserving of words you are about;
useful words that we may need,
need vitally, for
threatening times ahead?

WHINING

Whining, whining, whining
about the weeds swamping
the young cabbages, the slugs
ravaging the early lettuce,
and the raccoons prepping up
to raid the plums and grapes.
Inside the house, the dust rises
and settles, rises and settles,
and the cooking disappears daily,
and the linens need continually crisping,
and I've given up seeing clearly
through the windows darkly.
All this whining when
my husband appears in
my private writing area
to tell me that he has
just seen a family of quail,
scuttering about the wood yard.
The father on top of a pile of bark slabs
supervising, the babies running rampant.
Mother is to one side
pecking on clover. I sigh,
and give him a sweet smile
realizing there's things we neglect
to put into equations, when it comes to
whining.

knowing that
all things must pass
yet
a dying bed of purple crocus
is an infinitely sad thing

the robins
race me down
the rows
I seed, they peck
I seed, they peck,

we catch a visitor
cutting a flowering quince branch
it's irresistible
if it wasn't our tree,
we'd be stealing one too

long ago summers . . .
linen dresses, flat-soled shoes
the gentle sound
of croquet balls in my imagination
always in my imagination

in summer
we girls would sit
on the promenade
criticizing passing women, yet oh,
how we longed to be them

AMORPHOUS ME

I am a creature lacking edges;
my boundaries are ill-marked,
so I confuse myself easily
with others' wealth and fame,
with others' beauty spots.
In moments of euphoria
at small successes,
I threaten to disappear
in that thin line that borders
sea and sky, and,
in fits of melancholy
at a rejected haiku,
I curl up tight inside
the closest cloud.
At such times, only
the promising plum blossom
and the neighbor's ginger cat
sitting on our front-door mat
peering insightfully in
through the glass pane
restore me to solidity.

COMPLETE STORIES

There are no complete stories
in my life, no place where
I can point a finger and say
"This is where it began."
Then move my finger and say
"This is where it ended."
As the years go by, the stories soften
and change sequence, so what seemed
like a commencement, on closer look
becomes a closure, and what I think
may be coming, has already taken place.

FAMILY TANKA

the relief
of acknowledging
I'm not
the genius my mother
thought I was

my mother
sat by the fire removing
psoriasis scales
the smell of singed chicken
and I'm back there with her

two young girls
arms scratched with brambles
seated side-by-side
on father's crazy-pavement doorstep
made for just such wild women

and through the mirror
at the end of the bed she sees
her baby's head crowning
and quickly prays for its future
in this world of foolishness

A nearly perfect rose
for my nearly perfect arrangement
to accompany
a nearly perfect meal, at which
my husband sits reading at the table

the eighteen-month
goes tippy-toe to view
his new sister
his brows wrinkle in confusion
at what her arrival might mean

the photo is faded
but how can I forget
his small face
looking so trustingly
up to my own

seeing
parents with children
I breathe in guilt . . .
not that I didn't want to be a mother,
just not to be one every day

the afternoon couch
the perfect place to hate
one's parents
dredge up the past and
blame it on someone

the first time
my two small children
spoke to each other
without me being needed . . .
a startling moment

my total life
a brief shadow flickering
across the moon

GURUS

On first meeting the Rinpoche,
I bowed down in awe
at his eating of a peach;
no drop of juice ran down
his hand, his wrist, his arm,
as when I ate one.
Later I tried to change
his way of wiping his nose
on his robe, and gave to him
pure linen handkerchiefs
that he patted as they sat
packaged beside his filthy robe
during discourses.
The other day I watched
my husband of forty years
eat a mango with equal care
as the Rinpoche ate his peach and
marveled at the stupidity
of my years of guru-bowing-down,
and my stupidity that in
my forty years of marriage,
I had only just now recognized
my own mango-eating Rinpoche.

WASHING THE SIDING

Today we washed the siding
of our little vinyl cottage.
We worked together, as a team,
perfectly coordinated, moving
as one, as I soaked, he scrubbed,
I rinsed.
It was as if our breathing came
from one set of lungs, our arms
moved from one four-armed creature.
The spray, the foam, the spray . . .
It was as if we were making love,
but even better, for afterwards,
as we panted with exhaustion
from our efforts, we had the added bonus
of looking in pride at
our very clean vinyl-sided cottage.

DRUMBEG PARK

end of summer
pinned to the park notice-board
a bikini top

two children
building a sand-castle
tide turning
do all ventures get swamped
by the waves then, eventually?

Drumbeg meadows
camas, daisies, spring gold
I'm losing count . . .
the old farm cherry tree
scatters petals over them all

otters, seals, eagles,
Drumbeg is too much
for a single haiku
I spill over into tanka
with sandpipers and herons

tide pools
when the tide withdraws
a certain sadness
hangs around the stranded sea-weed
and the hermit crab carting his home

summers long ago,
before sunscreen was invented,
when we got burned
and peeled long strips of skin
from each other's backs

what
are sandwiches
without sand?
the sea-breeze lifts
the edge of the picnic cloth

full moon . . .
on the road-side bushes
shriveled rose hips

autumn wind
the used-clothing store
full of Halloween costumes

three lonely things—
an autumn's bare branch
the owl's call
the ribs of an old boat
covered in barnacles

heavy frost
in the white crocus
a sleeping bee

HOMETOWN—BLACKPOOL

I was raised in a honky-tonk town,
where life was a roller-coaster ride in which
screaming laughter covered infinite terror
and absolute absurdity; each resident
a side-show freak (when examined minutely),
worthy to be shown next to a five-legged sheep
or a sculpture of Jacob wrestling an angel . . .
all on that golden mile of coarseness.
It was a childhood struggling
with the paradox of a seaside town
with freezing waters. Waters that crashed
over the streetcar tracks and
had us running for cover.
A town pervaded with the constant smell
of cockles and whelks and cod and chips
wrapped in pages from the *News of the World*.
A *News of the World* kind of town, itself
wrapped in the vulgar, and tied with perverse
sexuality, where dirty postcards hung
in racks next to stands of Blackpool rock
and combs with your name on them.
On its three piers were slot machines, where
a metal hand would perhaps pick up a glass ring.
There third-rate comics laughed at their own jokes and
dusty blonds showed what was left
of their weary bodies.
From such a base, how could I grow up
to be anything more than trivial and cynical;
recording human follies, my writing dampened
with bittersweet tears.

DEATH VERSE

a friend's death . . .
the maple leaves are falling
too early this year

at the wake
I listen to the praise
and wonder
if we speak well of everyone
what value is the "well" we speak of?

the mist lifts
then falls again only
to clear later
intimations of death have come
and come again these last few years

the day
after he died
she started
to wear his old sweater
the bottom edge unraveling

listening to
the voice of the hospice worker,
he suddenly
realizes that it is he
who is dying

"ON DIAGNOSIS" TANKA

on diagnosis
time changed for her
each moment
became the only one and
each space stretched to the horizon

as pain
invaded her life
and only then
she realized a certain meaning
that gave sense to nonsense

plans and goals
disappeared with fatigue
all that was left . . .
a vague sense of self and
of the seasons passing

all she knew
was one anxiety
the anxiety
that maybe she had never been true,
true to herself that is

on diagnosis
we rush around
nudging our lives . . .
doing something makes
most things bearable

THE REMAINS OF THE DAY

I need my energy for dying
I cannot spare it
for entertaining folks
coming to see me die;
nor for folks trying to delay
my dying with pills and lotions
and various prescriptions.
Nor will I have energy
for folks coming to gloat
that their bodies are still intact,
while mine decays rapidly.
Nor energy to waste
on folks who are going to miss me
too much because they
have invested too much
in having me around.
In fact, as my days close,
I would like to be lying
in my favorite bed,
with the light filtering in
through gauze curtains
that blow gently in the breeze,
reminding me of the passing seasons.
The Trout Quintet would be playing
in an endless loop on the CD player
and *Pride and Prejudice* would be running
endlessly on a DVD player and
on my bedside table
The Remains of the Day.

it's happened!
we must be truly old . . .
sounds
of our neighbor shoveling
our driveway

when one
picks one's nose
it's so surprising . . .
things feel so large when hidden
so trivial when revealed

how varied
are our ways of surviving . . .
one person
carves small legends on a pole
another writes of turtle swamps

some say nothing costs
more and yields less benefit
than revenge,
but I think the enemy fallen
is a sight sometimes worth seeing

the sounds
of children plittering
through the fall leaves
even decay and loss
can have moments of joy

ikebana
is too much trouble . . .
like life
it needs renewing each day
and will be wilted by evening

my houseguest
relentlessly helpful
smiles me
into a fatigue
way beyond tiredness

POET LAUREATE
OF NANAIMO

2014–16

THIS MORNING

This short poem is engraved on a paving
stone set outside the entrance to the
Port Theatre in Nanaimo. It marks the
beginning of the Poet Laureate's walk.

this morning
an early phone call
and my life
commits deeper to the play
of black words on white paper

ME AND ALICE MUNRO

We had both decided,
(that is, Alice Munro and I)
that it was time to put down our pens,
cease the flow of words
that previously had come endlessly . . .
put it all to an end, when suddenly,
almost without warning,
and yet vaguely expected,
we both get a phone call.
Hers is from Sweden, while mine
is from Nanaimo,
(a little closer to home, I must admit).
Nevertheless, we both hear a phone ring.
Alice's call is to announce
that she has won a Nobel prize,
while mine is to announce
my poet laureate-ship of a small city.
A slice more modest I must admit,
yet still an honor, although
with an honorarium 1,000th the size.
But let's not dwell on such sordid matters
as that, let's just say that we,
(Alice Munro and I) have lived out
similar triangles, similar in angles,
but with sides not to be compared.
My tiny-sided triangle, though similar
to Alice's, reflects my comparative talents.
I have always sat comfortably with small,
knowing it is similar to large, but
sufficient in itself.

IF NANAIMO WROTE ITS MEMOIRS

November 18, 2014—My introduction to his Worship, the Mayor, and the Nanaimo City Council

When a city writes its memoirs
it is no different from you and I
writing ours.
We tend to rest on moments of glory
as the city would—
on the opening of a new mine,
or the movement of shipping.
Times for dancing at the waterfront,
or gathering in the park.
When a city writes its memoirs,
it does so, as we do ours, with
the distortions of fair-ground mirrors,
the trimmings of a topiary bush,
and all the tricks that looking backwards plays.
When a city writes its memoirs,
it is as if it is drawing up a ledger,
here red ink, here black, and
here a blurring of the two.
Yet the reckoning must be done
(as we too should evaluate our own years).
And when it is, no lingering
in the nostalgia of good times,
or the festering bitterness of regrets.
No, then is the time to turn to
a fresh page, a page full of promise
as to where the city (and we) might go next.

THANK YOU FRENZY

Thank you Poetry Gabriola
and the League of Canadian Poets
for keeping the wolf from the door;
and to the Sounder for touting
such writing skills as I have;
and to the CBC for allowing my voice
to occasionally get on the air;
and to the folks who come to my workshops,
for they helped pay the mortgage;
and the folks who come to my readings
who keep me alert so that
I can keep them alert;
and thank you to the folks who buy my books
and even the folks who don't buy my books
but borrow them from the library;
and to the folks who stand around in bookstores
reading my books, thank you for
putting them back on the shelves with
their front covers facing outwards,
instead of just showing the spine,
for they too do me a service;
and thanks to my twin who is often
unwittingly the butt of my wit and
to my daughter who lays out my books
when she feels like it, although I remind her
that I had to change her diapers
whether I felt like it or not;
and thanks to my son who calls on birthdays
and the day after Mother's Day
with a few welcome words;

and thanks to my husband,
who criticizes many aspects
of my being; thus keeping me
in the "here and now"
when I tend to stray to other times,
so that I can remember details
such as the fact that he prefers the toilet paper
be placed so that the paper rolls from the front
rather than from the back; but will put
up with it pulling from the back, so long as
I am consistent, which I am not;
and a thank you to my lucky stars
(whatever Cancer with Cancer rising
and my moon in Virgo might mean);
and from the stars it's a mere hop,
skip, and jump to thanking the galaxies
and the ends of the Universe, where apparently
the Big Bang is to be followed
endlessly by the Big Crunch,
meanwhile providing me with
just the right amount of oxygen
and just the correct degree of gravity
to allow me to sit on the deck
musing on life and writing poetry
of modest significance.
Thank you.

THE PROBLEM OF WRITING ABOUT P. K. PAGE

An evening in her homage given by the Crimson Coast Dance Society

Poets like to make lists.
It's a well known fact.
Lists of things they love—
the falling autumn leaves,
a misty morning,
the first ripe grapes on the vine.
And lists of things they hate—
inequalities, injustices, an Ontario winter.
But if I made a list
of all the many talents of P. K. Page,
it would overflow my usual haiku,
and spill over my 5-line tanka.
Even a sonnet would not suffice
to sing her praises.
But since I rarely exceed 14 lines
in my eccentric verse,
it seems I will have
to tumble and stumble outside
my comfort zone as I extol
this wondrous woman's works.
Poet, novelist, essayist, journalist,
librettist, artist and almost
every other "ist" you can think of.
But it is in her poem "Planet Earth"
that she speaks most clearly to me,

for it is a poem for a domestic reader
such as myself, as it tells of
needing to iron the earth,
wash the trees, loving the planet
as a laundress loves her linens,
smoothing the holy surfaces.
Ah ! It is only a poet such as she,
who is able to hallow the everyday
in this way, making the ordinary
extraordinary in her kaleidoscopic vision.

IMMIGRATION

February 15, 2014—Citizens' New Immigrant Reception

Why did we leave our birth land
you and I?
Crossing borders always means a loss—
a loss of family and friends
and the familiar that so comforts . . .
but does it?
Perhaps our move was rather to gain—
to gain the right to speak more freely;
to worship, or not, as we wished;
to live where we choose and not
be pushed into ghettos
made by others' prejudices.
Or perhaps we chose this country
for its clean air and clean water
and lakes and rivers stocked with fish,
and forests, forests, forests.
This country of peace-keepers,
not war-mongers.
A country that promised shelter
and the nourishment that
fresh opportunities offer,
and the encouragement of skills
and the possibilities that
new views present.
And in this country you and I have chosen,
we were both drawn to the West,
following past pioneers.
For here on this temperate island
in the Salish Sea,

we can find fertile soil
in which to set root.
And on this island, we have settled
in a harbor that can protect
and watch us flourish, a harbor
where perhaps we can set anchor
and be at rest.

YEAR'S END LEDGER

Yes, the year
had its good days—
the first shoots of green
up through the earth;
the first buds, then blossoms,
then fruit to be harvested;
the times of laughter and
warm skin touching warm skin.

Then there were the dismal days
of endless rain on skylights,
when nothing seemed to matter,
and things we once thought important
no longer seemed so.
And days far worse—
days of difficult diagnoses
and friends gone (some in a flash,
and some slowly day by day).
These personal moments
mere slivers of a troubled world.

And so we balance the year's pluses
with its minuses, and make our vows
that next year we will
do this and this, and not do
that and that,
in the fond hopes
that if not fame and fortune,
at least next year's ledger will
bring us a fine balance.

POETS ON THE WHOLE

There seems to be such a big gap between the
great poetry poets write and the wretched lives
they live. Here's a bit of advice for you:

I don't recommend
befriending a poet.
They are, on the whole,
unpleasant people.
They live life to excess
and can break you open
with a few well-chosen words
(not to mention what is in
the space between the lines).
Worse still, they can stab you
with an invisible stiletto
should you dare to
interrupt them while
they are reading in public.

THE USES FOR POETRY

April 28, 2014—The Mayor's Challenge

Your Worship and fellow Councilors I am delighted that you have taken up the Mayor of Regina's challenge to have a poet read to you during poetry month, April, and in recognition of World Poetry Day, March 21st (well, better late than never).

I'd like to start by telling you the reason I think poetry is useful:

Who has not
at times of distress
sighed, groaned, cried
and let out an anguished
"Why?"
And at such times,
who has not written
"Why?" down a hundred times
and followed with
a plea of some kind
to make the trouble go away?
And, as the distress
takes form on paper,
who has not added
an urgent call for help?
In this way poems are made.
And when the first robin returns
and the first green shoots
pierce through the earth,
who has not,
at such times,

sung out with optimism
that all will be well
with the earth someday,
and that lovers will find each other
and that neighborhoods will flourish?
At such times,
who doesn't jot down a line
to record pleasure
at cool, clear mornings,
and radiant sunsets?
And perhaps a word, or two
is added to the page
that this day might possibly
turn out better than others?
And so, we find,
that in our joy
a poem has been born.
Yes,
at such bitter and such sweet times
poetry has its uses, I find.

DO NOT WRITE POEMS

Do not write poems
of brilliant clarity
else they will enable
you to dine with kings
and mix with members
of the government.
Soon the Mafia
will be surrounding
and protecting you,
and the paparazzi
will encounter you
at breakfast ... and
you'll never be able
to write a poem
of brilliant clarity
again.

THE FULLNESS OF CANADA

July 1, 2014—Canada Day, Maffeo-Sutton Park

Have you ever thought
of the immensity of Canada?
Why, even looking at a map,
I have to swivel my head
from the left to the right.
It cannot all be taken in
at one glance, for
bracketed side to side
by crashing waves,
the endless prairies,
the infinite forests,
the craggy mountains,
the northern tundra . . .
everything is of an extreme.
The geography is unreal
in its immensity.
No wonder we Canadians
huddle together at the 49th parallel,
only a few of us brave enough
to venture farther north.
Perhaps its vastness
requires we Canadians to be
a little hesitant, somewhat tentative, eh?
Our moderation seems so reasonable though,
since we live in such a vast domain.

A GOOD STORY

*July 12, 2014—Opening of the Nanaimo North Branch of
the Vancouver Island Regional Library*

No matter how Facebook
exposes our lives, and
bloggers, too numerous to count,
may fill us in with more details
of theirs than
we really need to know,
there are still small children
drawing close to someone
reading from a book,
with their young voices asking urgently,
"And then . . . ? and then . . . ?
What happens next?"
They're just following
a good story, heedless
of the fact that it is
teaching them how to live—
how actions produce results,
and how we all go out on quests
for impossible things.
And we readers,
don't we love to group together
discussing tales, as if they were
our own reality,
the book of the month as if it were
our own concern?
And don't we punctuate our earnestness
with references to local gossip

and the nibbling of home-made cookies
and the pouring of freshly made tea?
Child or adult,
don't we marvel at the tellings of
the doings of others,
sometimes allowing their extremes
to nudge our own lives a little;
the power of a good story
transforming our own.

CELEBRATING THE VIEX

August 15, 2014—Vancouver Island Exhibition, on the 120th anniversary of the exhibition, and the 100th anniversary of the Canadian 4H clubs, that are so much a part of VIEx.

It seems these days
we are all rushing forward
without a thought,
Tweeting, Facebooking,
and blogging our lives away.
Time to step back
for a few days,
remembering in gratitude
where our food comes from,
and recalling the down-home
things our forebears did—
the canning, the quilting,
the soap and candle-making,
the pie-making, the carving,
the logging, the tilling,
the barn-raising, and, best of all,
the harvesting.
Exhibition time is time to celebrate
our roots in this land
and give thanks to those
who each year stir those memories
by bringing us reminders of
things we need to keep close with us—
the good things of what weren't always
the good old days—
children's eyes sparkling

as chicks hatch, and calf and colt
rise wobbling on their new legs;
the satisfaction of a pantry full
of home-made jams and pickles, and
a kitchen hung with braids of garlic;
the weary limbs resting
after a harvest brought in well.
All these things come to mind
as we wander the exhibition grounds
with the sounds of the Midway
familiar in the background,
and the smell of cotton candy
and popcorn penetrating.
And we don't search for
what is bigger and better,
but see everywhere that
talents are honored
even in the smallest endeavor.
Yes, that is what the Ex
is all about—
our caring, supporting and
encouraging our community,
our keeping our feet firmly
on the soil that feeds us,
while our imaginations soar
to the good that only we
can bring about.

ON THE BENCH

January 19, 2015—My presentation to the new mayor and council.

I am eating a double-scoop waffle-cone
on a bench by the seaplane dock.
I leisurely watch Nanaimo
amble by before my eyes—
dog-owners and their pets—
how like each other they grow
as they age together.
And families—
the youngest riding dad's shoulders,
the next holding her mother's hand and
always the dawdler who
straggles behind, picking the odd weed
to make a bedraggled bouquet.
And then there are the lovers . . .
entwined to various degrees.
And, at the dock, I watch the travelers
with their airport bags and backpacks.
And I wonder what images of Nanaimo
are tucked in their luggage,
and what Nanaimo memories
have slipped in for them
to unpack later.

WHAT A POEM CAN DO

April 20, 2015—The Mayor's Challenge

A poem
is a strange thing . . .
it's not prose
describing an event,
commenting philosophically
on the state of the world,
or telling of love, or the lack thereof.
And yet a poem
can do all these things,
and more.
For it can condense matter,
distill the essence,
purify the messy,
congeal the scattered.
Each word of a poem
can carry the weight
of the universe within it,
and one small verse
can bring a new world
out of a black hole,
or tip the present one
over the event horizon,
or tell of an early snowdrop,
its petals marked with green.

THE USES OF POETRY: THE MUNICIPAL REPORT 2015

The first request by the city for 2015 was
an unusual one. It was for a poem for the
foreword of the Annual Municipal Report.

It's true—
one cannot eat poetry,
nor can it be used
as a roof over one's head,
or as clothing, or herbal cure.
And yet, without poetry,
perhaps we would not linger
quite so long
under spring blossoms;
nor give time to float
for a while in summer waters,
admiring the clouds
feathering the bluest sky;
nor crunch the autumn leaves
underfoot, with the glee
of a small child;
nor stand at the window
watching the first snowfall,
while asking ourselves
important questions that have
no answers.
Poetry intensifies how we see,
how we smell, how we hear,
how we touch, how we taste—

allowing us fresh ways
to view this troubled world.
Poetry allows us to get up
in the morning with a certain courage
to meet the contingencies
of the everyday.

THE BLANK PAGE

April 9, 2015—Cultural Awards' night at the Port Theatre

In the beginning is a blank page . . .
then the first line of a poem appears,
the first rough brushstrokes,
the first few notes hung on a staff,
a couple of footprints, first steps in a new dance.
Where have they come from?
There was nothing on the page
and now there is something—
a miracle in a way, yet one in which
we seem to have taken part—
our pen stroke, our brush on the paper.
Yet if we're asked to do it on demand,
often the pen stumbles, the brush hesitates
as though we're waiting on our Muse to inspire.
Yet other times, we mark the page boldly
as if to arrogantly declare, "Look at me!
I've scaled Mount Olympus and stolen, for a moment, the
creative power of the gods."
I'm told creative energy
jumps from neuron to neuron
via the synapses,
but how does all that bouncing energy
manifest as—
"I wandered lonely as a cloud
that floats on high o'er vale and hill."
How does all that speeding energy
become the Mona Lisa?
And how does that almost faster-than-light
energy wind up as "Your Cheatin Heart?"

They're the same questions I've been asking
since I was a small child.
If you have a reasonable answer
as to what the creative process is,
please don't hesitate to e-mail me
immediately so that I can sort out
what I've been doing these last twenty years,
and whether my life adds up to more than
just a small sigh.

NANAIMO BOUND

The Hub City we're called.
And more people come to Nanaimo
by ferry, plane, boat, or car
and leave Nanaimo by similar methods
in a week than actually live here.
Just think of that.
It's as if a whole town
arrived and departed within days
leaving a few plastic cups
and foam clamshells on the sidewalks.
Supposing we could halt them
midway between arrival and departure . . .
persuade them to stay, settle down,
rent a condo, send their kids to school,
buy season tickets at the Port Theatre,
we'd have doubled the town overnight.
But let's not even think of it.
Let's hurry them on their way,
bid them a speedy "Adieux"
along with a suggestion
that they make a quick stop
at a downtown restaurant
to drop some money into the economy
as they pass through.
I'm a small city girl,
comfy with small houses,
local stores, and familiar faces.
Even in her imagination, a small city girl
needs to keep her small city, small.

THE MAYOR'S CHALLENGE

I picture the mayors and councilors
all across Canada
sitting in bewilderment,
(not having had poetry read to them
since high school days)
as poets rant politically,
or spiritually, or praising
the domestic hearth, or vilifying it.
The TV camera slowly passes across
the mayor and councilors' faces,
and some look bored, or have
their eyes closed, thinking about
the other items on the night's agenda.
But then you'll see
the odd mayor or councilor
startled to full attention
by some devastating or
appealing line of verse.
Their eyes may well be filling
up with tears, that they hastily
cover up by blowing their noses loudly.
But one can't deny it,
it's there for all to see . . .
the moment when the power of poetry
meets a receptive ear.
At such a moment, all is in full flow
and the Mayor's Challenge has been met.

SPRING FEVER

May 1, 2015—Cascadia Poetry Festival 3, welcoming Cascadia poets to Nanaimo

Another rainy day
on the West Coast and
I am requested to write
an upbeat poem, full
of the promise of spring,
the flowing from the thaw.
But words are not flowing
from my pen, which stumbles
awkwardly across the page
wanting to note down
the weight of a sad body,
the strictures of an aging mind.
I seize the pen firmly
and strike across the pathetic
beginnings of a new poem.
"Now," I tell it, "Now write
'joyful,' and 'greening,'
and 'sprouting,'
and link them together
in some sparkling fresh way.
And for a coda, note
that old age brings pluses and minuses
into balance, and that even
the moss on a West Coast roof
can harbor small lively insects."

A JUST-RIGHT COUNTRY

July 1, 2015—Canada Day in Nanaimo

When one thinks of Canada
one thinks of hockey, and maple syrup,
the beaver, the bear, and the white-tailed deer,
the trillium, the dogwood, the maple leaf . . .
One doesn't think of the extremes
of brash America, nor the heavy weight of
history-loaded Europe.
We are a Goldilocks country,
somewhere between a melting pot
of immigrant cultures and
the tribalism that separates.
We are a "just right" country
united by our awesome land—
from sea to sea to shining sea.
For if we have extremes, it is
in those endless Prairies,
those snow-peaked Rockies,
those forever forests of pine
and spruce and fir, and
those waters crashing our boundaries.
But within, we are a people of the middle way;
somewhat hesitant, loathe to extol our virtues.
And, even in our cities, our small town values
are clearly signed.
In our humility, we can afford
to celebrate our abundance with
our generosity to others and with
a certain kindness to ourselves.

TREES AND POETS

September 3, 2015—Poems for the introduction to the show Silva at the Nanaimo Art Gallery

Poets understand trees.
Deciduous poets,
waver with the seasons.
In spring, their words burst forth,
as do the oak leaves,
full of hope and careless trust
in the coming year.
In summer, their words
hover in the solid heat,
and poets pause,
laden heavy with metaphors.
The trees too seem stilled
awaiting fruition.
In fall, their words sadden
at the bittersweetness of it all,
and the trees droop with
the heavy burden of fruit and nuts.
In winter, those deciduous poets hide,
rubbing the frosty pane
to clear a lookout hole
in order to say a few words about
piled snow and the barrenness of life.
The trees sway with the winter winds,
their silhouettes morphing into
skeletons and ghosts.
But we poets of the rain-coast forests,

trudge up and over
fallen branches of hemlock,
western red cedar, Pacific silver fir,
Sitka spruce and Douglas fir,
careless of our words as they tumble out,
anxious to find a trail to somewhere
to anywhere, as the mosses, ferns and lichens
festoon tree trunks and branches,
their fog-drip giving our verses
a heated, humid, jungle-like feel.
Standing snags . . . and we suffer writer's block.
But canopy openings, when found,
allow us the pause in our haiku,
the indent in our free verse.
We rain-coast poets stay verdant
and spew forth our wet, limpid verse
all year, assured that the forest
will be there to shelter and challenge us . . .
rather like a marriage.

THE USE OF TREES

Now for something a bit more practical—

For economic animals,
trees are a crop
to be sown and reaped
for lumber, cedar chests,
chopsticks, toothpicks,
guitars, baseball bats,
newspapers, and fuel
for our stoves and
a thousand other things.
Like the proverbial pig,
nothing goes to waste
save the soughing of
their branches in the wind.

For we romantics . . .
trees still our agitation
and silence our violence.
For us, they are continually green
reminding us of branches
climbed in childhood and
boughs laid under with our loves.

But left alone,
trees do just what
they are meant to do . . .
clean the air and purify the water,
home the birds and small creatures.

In autumn, their leaves and cones
nourish the forest floor,
and even when fallen and decayed,
they can still nurse young trees
that shoot up promisingly
from their grounded trunks.

THE FOREST FLOOR

And speaking of forest floors, here's a poem about the
"O" horizon. The O horizon has three distinct organic
layers: one of leaves, pine needles and twigs (Oi);
underlain by a partially decomposed layer (Oe);and
then a very dark layer of well decomposed humus (Oa).

Change happens
at the edge of things—
where sea covers sand,
or sun hits soil,
or even where sun does not hit soil,
but filters down slowly
through leaves and needles . . .
say on forest floors.
It's at these overlaps
things move from known to unknown,
from visible to invisible.
Decomposing, decomposing, decomposed—
leaves, needles, cones, twigs,
moss, lichen litter the ground.
Deer, fox, mouse leave
their feces, entrails, fur, bones.
Fungi, molds, bacteria,
slugs, snails, beetles, earthworms
set to work, 'til all that's left
are skeletons of once fleshed things.
And these too, in time, crumble to dust,
their origins lost.
For on the forest floor,
as elsewhere, death and decomposition
are necessary and inevitable.

Necessary to feed the soil
from which, in its optimistic time,
fresh life shoots forth
and the round is continued.

THE RIGHT SIZE

2016—Written for the annual gathering of the Royal Architectural Institute of Canada, Nanaimo

How we strain our necks
in awe of the sky scraping towers
of Dubai and Singapore and
Shanghai and Makkah.
Imagine staying on the 100th
floor of a hotel, why it would take
a chunk of our morning just to go
to our room for something we had forgotten.
The proud architects
have almost overcome gravity
as they defy the heavens
with their wondrous efforts.
Yet, neck strain is neck strain
and for us small town folks
we smile with content
at neighborhoods where
we can call each shop-keeper by name,
and they know ours' too,
and where we can look out
for each other's backs
as our front yards blend
and our backyards host babies,
and young lovers and mid-life crises
and the swinging of swings
and the rocking of rocking chairs.
We want our workplace to
enhance our days and

our homes to welcome us back
as shadows deepen.
And yes, our homes should
overlook greenery and have paths nearby
for an evening stroll,
and benches for watching
the passing crowd.
But working or playing,
we want our buildings to
lean us towards contentment,
just ample,
knowing sufficient is enough.
Let others aspire to the heights.
We small town folks
cling to our neighborhoods
to give us a setting and a settling
and a satisfactory sigh.

NEW POEMS

CELEBRATION

I forgot my husband's birthday this year,
and we both forgot the anniversary
of our wedding.
I have only one grandchild,
but barely managed to remember
his birthday the day before.
So thank God for Amazon and
its instant gift certificates.
We are not a Hallmark family.
We let Valentine's Day and Mother's Day
float past untended.
We celebrate in small,
often silent ways without
toasts with champagne,
or bold and lying speeches.
We celebrate the image
of leaf shadow on leaf,
the small, perfect nest
of a paper wasp,
the first hummingbird of the year,
the gasp for opening forsythia,
a harvest basket of our ripe plums,
a quiet moment when the power is out
and we lie together listening
to Golden Oldies on our solar radio.
Small moments of celebration,
but celebration none the less.

THE SEASONS

he calls his dog back
she, her child ... impossible
on this spring day

seed-exchange time
how conscious we are
of heritage plants
as we search the table for
grandmother's favorite bean

weeding the path
on my kneeling pad
I feel
I am doing penance
on the way to Lhasa

heat wave
the coolness of clouds
across the moon

swimsuits on the line
sand on the kitchen floor
my endless summer guests

parched summer
the hard shadow of a fig tree
shifts slightly in the wind

autumn
the ground russet with
scattered leaves
big plans wind down
and dreams grow smaller

after twenty years
our first walnut crop . . .
squirrel on the branch

white on white
the dazzling of first snowdrops
through melting snow

heavy frost
in the white crocus
a sleeping bee
I sort out my seed packages
anxious for spring

NOEL REPLAY

The first Noel
was simple.
Cold there was,
and stars,
and shepherds adoring and
wise men bringing gifts.
But, as years went by,
in the annual celebration,
the gifts and food
outshone the stars . . .
the stuffed turkey,
the Brussels sprouts,
the plum pudding with
a sprig of holly stuck in it,
and the presents gaudily
wrapped under the tree
took precedence.
Occasionally the odd child
would look enraptured
out the frost drawn window
searching the sky
for a particular star.
Or, when opening its gifts,
the child would think
of the three wise men
coming from far off
to adore the infant, and
then, after that moment,
carefully, that child
would open an old box
and set out
the Nativity scene

with well-worn figures—
placing the model sheep and cattle
around the baby as it lay
in its cradle promising
peace to the world.
And then the child would place
the mother and father close by.
The father looking on,
trusting the infant would bring
joy to all mankind.
The mother fearful, as all mothers are,
for the baby's future.
Yes, it is such children as this one
that in their innocence,
replay that first Noel
as it should be remembered each year.

LOVE

letters once
carved on bark
now grown faint . . .
is love so fugitive then
love that was once so incisive?

telling you
of my love, you bend down
to kiss me . . .
it's all so easy; why didn't
I think to do it days ago?

early morning
we lie together
no desire
yet something better . . .
the comfort of each other

first garden strawberry
we divide it carefully
for dessert . . .
such division only
brings us closer

my intuition
your reasoning
two ways to look at reality . . .
on cold nights how
we cling together

if only
we could see things
as for the first time . . .
I glance at my husband
reading at the breakfast table

marriage
settles in comfortably
like old slippers . . .
but oh for fresh love running
hand in hand in the rain

harlequin couple
paddling out into the bay
their wakes crossing . . .
I quickly count
our years together

the lies
we tell each other, side by side
in the summer sun
we cannot repeat under the covers;
the skin on skin of winter nights

how can your truth
be my truth?
you get restless
as I linger over a print
at the art gallery

—continued

a bench under the grape vine—
a birthday offering
from my husband
countering my years of ups and downs
he made sure it was level

like wood shavings
on the workshop floor
we curl tightly together
the warmth of skin on skin
our long time comfort

sometimes
my husband seems as if
from some alien planet . . .
when I am bored with life
he is there—new and strange

saying "sorry" before bed
I remember my mother
advised this

FUGITIVE PAINT

Is love then a fugitive paint?
The reds blackening and
the blazing sunsets darkening.
The pink haze of meeting
becoming the white of mourning,
and the blues ever deepening and
enveloping the canvas.

HUMAN NATURE

the children
tumble down the hillside
shrieking with laughter
laughter enough to push
the clouds higher in the sky

The young girl
goes down to the beach
with her book
hoping for new experiences
as she turns the pages slowly

women together
our kimono sleeves
don't brush by chance

even with a familiar venture
how we hesitate on the edge
fearful, yet eager

how we want
to encapsulate life
dip it in formaldehyde
pin it in a box so it will stay
as we want it forever

his tragic crash
headlines for two days
then is displaced
by a campus rape
and life continues

five things that hold me—
a child swinging through a spring breeze,
a parent bundling a child into a snow suit,
two soon-to-be-lovers touching hands,
an aged couple loading a car with groceries,
an old man staring out at nothing.

in the ambulance
my first responder tells me
all his troubles

in the doctor's office
"ONE ISSUE PER PATIENT" . . .
I start to stammer

TANKA OF EXILE

in exile
we make myths
of our homeland
poised uncertain between
assimilation and return

searching for a home
other than in our own heart
is perilous
must we always keep
our suitcase packed?

our past
is layered thickly
with people and places . . .
only looking back can
we see patterns in the journey

we move
from one age
to another
our life from birth to death
a continual diaspora

the rich textures
of our lives entrap us
into believing
we are solid, when we are
just stitched lightly together

HEARTSONG CHOIR

A Gabriola women's choir led by Jen Turner

Year after year,
I watched their earnest faces,
looking for a matching intensity
in my own.
I heard their voices raised in hope,
while listening to the beating within
of my own feeble heart.
I watched their shining smiles
and tentatively touched
my own lips for any sincerity
that might be there.
I felt enfolded in their community,
as they sang as one being.
And each year I felt tears
come to my eyes as they sang
of yearnings unknown to me
with such honesty and
with such trust.

DUKKHA

My DNA is crammed
with thousands of years
of persecution and pograms,
of expulsions and
lives lived in perpetual exile,
so when I hear
of injustice anywhere
(as large as genocide, or
as small as one neighbor
maligning another),
immediately my cells
line up in indignation
and words of protest
overwhelm my mind.
The headline read
"Man Kills Boy."
No, let me correct that,
"White Man Kills Indigenous Youth."
Yes, that's the trigger,
the trigger that floods
me with images
of Inca-killing Spaniards,
of Leopold's slaughter in the Congo,
of Mao and Stalin and Pol Pot,
the Armenians, Rwanda, Srebrenica,
the Kurds, the Isaaqs, the Rohyingya,
and here and there and everywhere
the indigenous people of those lands,
and for all times and all places
always the Jews, the perpetual Jews . . .

The snapshots pale, and
I am left, once more,
with the stark image
of one white man killing
one indigenous youth.
An image that may well
tear a country in shreds.
And, uncertain what to do,
I turn to my husband,
who answers my unspoken question
in his usual simple way.
"Life is complex,"
is what he says.

READING, WRITING, AND OTHER ARTS

a new year
always promises
better than the last
blank paper on the easel
fresh brushes placed ready

poets make lists
trying to put the world
in order
things useful, things beautiful,
things reminding us that all passes

when gardening
I arrange my rows
like lines of writing
neat and precise, but allowing
for the occasional rebel seed

why waste energy
fretting about the world
a poem written
in the early hours
and I'm in balance all day

doing good
may be doing good
or may be harmful,
but a good poem is
always a good poem

poets notice things
new cushions in others' houses
first grapevine buds
the signs of friends aging
young spiders bursting their sack

"what's they for?"
one elderly woman asks
about the abstract sculptures . . .
I start to explain about the beauty
of form and how it can move us

flamenco isn't danced by
learning flamenco, flamenco is danced
by living flamenco
flamenco isn't Sophia Loren
flamenco is Anna Magnani

WRITING A TANKA

Writing a tanka
is like feeling
the breeze coming up
from the shore
on the first day of autumn.
It tells you that
the full blooming of summer
is over—
the seeds sown in spring
are now to be harvested,
and entropy moves center stage
as leaves fall and
stalks rot in the ground.
Yes, writing tanka
is like that.
Like a record of a full life
and the bittersweetness
of knowing that
it must come to an end.

WHY WE READ

We read to learn
that somewhere
good is rewarded and
evil punished.
We read to learn why
there is something
instead of nothing, and
why that something
forms our universe,
from the outer galaxies
to the daisies on the lawn.
We read of things past
that we might make use
of the lessons they teach us.
We read of possible
future times and
whether they might be closer
to Heaven than to Hell.
We read of the present and
how it shifts and shakes us.
We read to remind ourselves
that we already know
how life should best be lived,
but that we have, for a moment,
forgotten.
We read, most of all
to know that we are not alone.

ON WRITING MEMOIRS

the backward journey
may jog you forward
along the next trail

looking back,
all I see through
past mists
are two young girls
swinging dangerously high

searching for
some meaning in my life
all I find
are some faded photos
in a cookie tin

my memoirs written
I drop past images like
discarded clothes . . .
all save a schooner painting
hung over a distant fireplace

the sepia of
our histories . . .
things no longer
black and white or
sure of themselves

WHY WE SING

We sing because the morning's fine
and the afternoon suits our mood,
and we sing in the evening
because it's been a deserving day.
We sing in dark times to drum up courage
and in times of chaos in order
to find a way out.
We sing as we turn the soil,
and as we later gather the harvest.
We sing to proclaim brotherhood,
or sisterhood, or a sharing of humanity,
and we sing at the coming into life
and also at its departing.
Sometimes we sing for no reason at all,
just the sound rising up from deep within
and ourselves standing aside
to let the pure notes find their place.

ON THE WAY TO KINDERGARTEN

All the truths
of the universe
are contained
in this small body.
All the wisdom
of the sages;
all the knowledge
that science presents;
all the doings of humans,
both good and bad,
are in this small body
whose soft little hand
rests in mine
as we walk
to the school on
the first day
of kindergarten.

MY NATURE

the year
draws to a close
my "to do" list no shorter

alone at the window
I look outside
with no expectations

am I just
a will-o'-the-wisp
sewn together
from memories
and anticipation?

reading on the deck
my list of "to do" things
as a bookmark
the shadows lengthen
yet still I sit

every morning
the bedroom emerges
from the shadows
like a small but
miraculous birth

the man
I was obsessed with
so many years ago . . .
I can't remember his name or face
only the obsession

—*continued*

life is a twisted olive tree
I feel so useless today
no one needs me . . .
on such a day,
I hardly need myself

we all
wend our way home
in our own style . . .
I make a beeline
for the fast check-out

this sky
this earth
this human body
three things that
have me in awe

epiphanies
rarely last out
the week . . .
I wash the tines of a fork
very mindfully

the notice
on our door says
"walk in"
as I age "good" and "bad"
seem to have lost meaning

recalling the blame
and regrets of the past
doesn't help . . .
today I will spring-clean and
get rid of those cobwebs

every day
as night falls
I account for the day . . .
I clean my karma up
as I would the kitchen floor

I watch myself
nudge this way and that
as my senses input
I seem to have no life . . .
there is only the adjusting

PILGRIMAGE

I've been to the Himalayas
searching with one hundred thousand
full-length prostrations for roads
that led to Lhasa;
I've wandered the hills of the Lake District
seeking the magic words of distant poets
in the hopes that they would inspire
a few of my own;
I've sailed the oceans to find
even more distant seers,
myself in Zen robes, or covered
in the ribbons of secret initiations
or the beaded headdress of a temptress,
muttering a thousand mantra.

Yesterday, I paused at the step
of our small vinyl-sided cottage,
myself in gum-boots and
shabby garden clothes.
The smells from the kitchen
cheered my spirit
and glimpses of the well worn recycled furniture
appeased my Puritan instinct
and the pieces of our creative name
reminded me of the energies needed
to bring the golem to life . . .
and suddenly, aware of the wealth within,
I took my simple pilgrimage over the threshold.

TIDAL POOL TANKA

tidal pools
sand ripples, water ripples,
sunlight ripples,
what a fine piece of weaving
this beach has produced

a hermit crab
drags its home on its back
the length of the pool
our mortgage paid
I have no such burden

tidal pool
the barnacles kick open
one by one
I know they are feeding
but somehow I feel welcomed

high tide
the tidal pool disappears
water over water . . .
lost in the day's news
I await the tide turning

ON THE BENCH AT DRUMBEG PARK

My friend's father
never made it to the west,
although all his life
he'd longed for that coast
and the promise it held.
He'd not been the first to fail,
nor is he likely to be the last.
At his death, she had a bench placed
where he might have viewed
the Strait and the mountains beyond
and the dreams on the horizon
which may not have moved any nearer
even if he had made it to the west.
And when I sit on that bench,
I think, without regret, of things
that never came to fruition,
things that promised, and then turned away.
And gradually, sitting on that bench,
my past fades into the mist
on the far islands, and all I'm aware of
is the sun-warmed bench, and my
sun-warmed body, and
the healing power of Drumbeg.

alone
on the hospital gurney
I realize that
I've always been alone
even when I wasn't

after my twin left
I was so happy
in the womb
so happy, so happy,
until I wasn't

asleep
in his cot
unaware
of the risks he will take
my little gambler

awake at 7 am
I try to remember what
I had remembered at 3 am

SKYLIGHT TANKA

celebrating our new skylight handily
situated above the daybed

my daybed
lies under the skylight
I am an expert
on that small piece of sky
that it frames

high winds
at the blink of an eyelid
a new set of clouds
moves swiftly across the skylight
restless skyscape, restless me

the sun rises
high above the solitary pine . . .
I decide
to lie and watch it
labor across the sky

grey skylight
grey trees viewed
through it
grey me looking at
all this greyness

today the clouds
are many-layered . . .
as a child
I would lie and wonder
if God lived above the highest

the sun explodes
on the skylight . . .
I get distracted
by the smears my bad cleaning
has left across the glass

a turkey vulture
chases an eagle
across our skylight
is there no end to chasing
and being chased in this world?

the rain
shattering down
the skylight
the tall pine breaks
into a thousand shimmers

through
the skylight
the sky is grey—still
this strange lethargy
after a poem is done

the rising sun
breaks through
the skylight
I shut my eyes to its blare
and to the blare of life

LACKING DUENDE

It's not that I have
any problem with creativity—
my ideas come fast and furious,
linking in strange and exotic ways.
It's just that they do not
penetrate the bone to the marrow.
The soil I plant them in
is not sprinkled with blood . . .
My writing is of familiar ground
that lacks the suffering of the outcast,
the sorrows of the diaspora.
My words may circle
on the edge of the devilish,
but never plunge into the Hell states.
They lack the grit of downtown,
or the roughness of wilderness.
I tell the tales of a small-town girl
tinged with the longing to be noticed . . .
but not too much.
At my age, the presence of death
may shadow my every line,
but it is of death delayed,
not death imminent.
Not the kind of death a samurai
confronted as he stepped from home
not knowing for sure whether
he would ever return.
Yet still, my poetry is not without redemption.
I seek to find duende in the everyday—
a ball of twisted twine,
a worn-down kitchen spoon,

the many-times turned pages
of a beloved book.
And when I write of love,
although it is not of passion,
at least I remind that it can
never be truly happy.
As to quests and ventures,
I speak of them as futile, rather than heroic,
the grail always just beyond my reach.
I may have somersaulted the bull's back
in my "maybe" lines, but,
I have never closed in for
the final stabbing.

MY MODEL FARM

When I was young
I had a model farm—
the model sheep were
in their model pen;
the model pigs
in their model sty;
the model cattle
in their model barn;
and the model chickens
in their model coop.
The model ducks swam
on a mirror pond
that I polished every day.
The model farmer
was caught stilled
while tossing the hay
with a toy pitchfork,
while his model wife
was churning butter in
the model farm house.
Everything was as it should be.
I saw to that.
Later, I met up with reality—
the real reality of the farmer
who killed the cows and pigs and ducks.
Fences got broken and
horses ran loose.
The pond became overgrown
with pond weed and
the roof shakes blew off
in a storm and
a heavy snow downed the gutters.

The bank foreclosed
on the farm after
a couple of bad harvests.
All that I came to know,
and yet that small core,
a place where everything
was ordered, a perpetual
harvest time, where
fruit never decayed,
and plants never went
to seed too early;
a place where barns were clean,
and the kitchen was
continually stocked with
braids of garlic, and
jars of preserves;
where the farmer and his wife
never aged or
grew weary of each other,
that core stayed with me,
keeping me foolishly optimistic
when times were otherwise,
and keeping me stupidly stubborn
in the face of a depressing humanity.
We all need those cores
in what seems to be
a purposeless world,
where we understand so little . . .
the comings and goings
and the strange, impossible time
in between.

PLACES

over still waters
the shadow of a plane
imprints

blue sea, blue sky,
and in between
a small blue island

harbor lights
dim through the fog
the distant ship's horn

the small boat
pulled up on shore
oars somewhere else

a writer
demands a solitary life
why on earth
did I move to
the social whirl of Gabriola?

Drumbeg waters
the coldest on the island
yet gathering there
our warm friendship seems
to raise them a few degrees

islanders stake
their property lines
and fence them . . .
sometimes to keep out
sometimes to keep in

why
live on an island
if you complain
constantly about the ferry
whose schedule never fits ours

WHO CARES?

October 18, 2014, Gabriola Museum fundraiser

Who cares that
First Nations summer-camped
on the narrows?
Or that, when white settlers
came to this island
they took native wives as
partners in their ventures?

Who cares
that families cleared
crown grant land and
built their homesteads,
and planted crops
so that they could provide
and flourish?

Who cares that
it took five hours to row
to Nanaimo bringing
fruit and veg and lambs and pigs
to sustain the miners there?

Who cares that
the only teacher on the island
rowed to Victoria with
three of his students for their exams
and rowed back . . .
four teachers at the oars?

Who cares that
the islanders cut millstones,
and baked bricks and
built ships so that
fathers could sustain their families?
And that their wives baked and preserved
and scrubbed and helped in the fields
alongside their men, equal energy
in those pioneering days?

Who cares that
canoes and rowboats
moved to sailboats,
moved to gas boats,
moved to ferries
for the comings and goings of the island?

The museum cares
for it knows for sure
that if we don't well heed
our island's past,
we cannot well guide
our island's future.

SICKNESS, OLD AGE, AND DEATH

hand in hand
we now lie watching
other people's lives

the day
after he died
she cut up
his pajamas for use
to make rag rugs

when we're young
the whole world
is ours
as we age, the horizon
moves into our backyard

I grow old
impatient with words
which can explain nothing
"what is left to do?" I ask
the wind blows up from the beach

preparing
for my next step
in life
I am surprised to find
sickness, old age, and death

as I age
I seek perpetual
safeness
knowing that any life worth living
demands perpetual risk

growing old
is no guarantee
that foolish maidens
will turn to wise old crones
muttering oracles worth a dime

fretting about life
past regrets and future fears . . .
when past and future
suddenly collapse into chickadees
on the mountain ash

one person
if stubborn and focused
can turn things around
I idly flick the pages for role models
though at my age, maybe it's too late

at this age
when I have the urge
to try something new
I pause and realize
I have already done it

SHIFTING GRANITE

There stands the table base,
and fifty feet away stands
the granite top,
and somewhere between the two
stand you and I,
unwilling to admit
the frailty of our aging.
"We can do it,"
I say confidently,
stuck in the past
when our muscles built
a house together.
You hesitate . . .
then scuffing the slab
from side to side,
you get it close to
where it has to go.
"OK", I say, ever positive,
"One, two, three, lift."
But the granite remains
adamantly on the ground.
As is my wont,
I shoot from up to down
in an instant, and declare,
"We'll never do it!"
willing to give up
at the first attempt.
You think of one solution,
then another, chewing the problem
and unwilling to surrender,
but even together,

our weary bodies
can't lift the slab an inch
from where it stubbornly stands.
You finally declare,
"You and I can't do it."
I quickly agree, but
then you add,
"But you and I and gravity can."
And tipping the slab forward
you rest it slanted on
the table base.
And it is true, for in a flash
the granite morphs fairy-light,
and we lift it easily together
and slide it into place.
We stand triumphant,
as if we had peaked Everest
or swum the Channel.
In age, each small victory
demands its celebration.
And, as the victories get smaller,
we still pat each other
on the back,
remembering the successes
that have made up
our life together.

THE MEANING OF LIFE

we all
find the Gods that
will work for us.
I watch Virtue and Moir
glide across the ice

are we all
just eight-year-olds
watching
to see who gets more
hugs, presents, cakes?

what can be better
than finding something
that one has lost . . .
a sister, a lover, a library book,
or a spoon missing from a set?

interesting
things happen
at boundaries
soft and hard overlay
past and future held in the present

the bars
that restrain us
the bars that protect us
sometimes it's hard to tell
one from the other

meditation
is not about sitting
on cushions
it is about washing
the tines of a fork mindfully

on sewing a quilt
I prick my finger . . .
how imaginary
this thin life is,
yet, also very real

does creation
spring from chaos or
from the void?
I jot down a few words
about the heavy morning fog

WORKING THE LAND

First were the indigenous people,
gathering clams and oysters,
salal berries and wild garlic.
Then came the others, fleeing
the mills and mines of Britain, and,
loathe to enter the mines of Nanaimo,
they chose instead the toil
of logging the firs and pines,
and pulling the stumps, and
clearing the brush, providing
land for their sheep and cattle and pigs.
Cabins were built, and forges started up
to make shoes for their work horses.
The Grays, the Degnans, the Edgars,
The McGuffies, Hogans and da Silvas
settled in, and some married
First Nations' women who
knew well the ways of the land
and the surrounding waters.
And orchards flourished with
Gravensteins, Kings, and sour cherries.
And fields were planted with potatoes and beets,
and turnips, and rows of strawberries.
And these cleared fields
fed the families of Gabriola,
and also the settlers in Nanaimo;
the harvest rowed slowly over.
And looking back at their labors,
it's as if we can see their footprints
in our own tilled fields,
still see their harvests in our own.

AN ENDING

An ending
does not always
blend in smoothly
with a beginning.
Sometimes there is a pause.
Time to look back tenderly
before turning to step
over the threshold.
Sometimes the crack
at the doorstep seems
to open to a potential chasm;
causing one to teeter
for a moment,
with a small shudder of fear,
before one closes one's eyes
and giant steps over it,
not knowing yet
which direction needs to be taken.
Still, a walking away is inevitable,
even though small shards
and burrs of the last years
cling persistently to one.
And that is not altogether unwanted,
for scraps of things learned
and fragments of friendships made
can make a fine patchwork cloak
to warm us in new ventures
and protect us from the certain to happen frictions when
our old selves
morph into our new.

ENDPAPERS

at the clinic
I know everyone
in the waiting room ...
growing old together
we now share diagnoses

if only
an enlarged heart
meant more loving ...
I lie recalling
the folks I need to thank

we lie together
like a knight and his lady
in a tomb effigy ...
only the rise and fall of the covers
shows we are still of this world

a pile
of detective stories
by my chair
as if solving murders
can help me deal with death

opera singer?
chorus girl? mathematician?
artist?
finally I decide that
I'll come back as myself

looking back
I might have wished for
just the easy parts . . .
yet tough times opened me
to strengths I never knew

clouds move
across the skylight
I also drift along

ABOUT THE AUTHOR

Naomi Beth Wakan is the inaugural Poet Laureate of Nanaimo (2014–16) and the Federation of British Columbia Writer's Inaugural Honorary Ambassador. She has published over fifty books. Her most recent book of essays, *On the Arts*, came out in 2020 (Shanti Arts). Her trilogy, *The Way of Tanka, The Way of Haiku*, and *Poetry That Heals* was published by Shanti Arts in 2019. Wakan is a member of The League of Canadian Poets, Haiku Canada, and Tanka Canada. She lives on Gabriola Island, British Columbia, Canada, with her husband, the sculptor Elias Wakan. www.naomiwakan.com

Shanti Arts

Nature · Art · Spirit

Please visit us online
to browse our entire book
catalog, including poetry collections
and fiction, books on travel, nature,
healing, art, photography, and more.

Also take a look at our highly
regarded art and literary journal,
Still Point Arts Quarterly, which
may be downloaded for free.

WWW.SHANTIARTS.COM

www.ingramcontent.com/pod-product-compliance
Lightning Source LLC
Chambersburg PA
CBHW070329090426
42733CB00012B/2412